Animals of the World

Koala

By Edana Eckart

Children's Press®
A Division of Scholastic Inc.
New York / Toronto / London / Auckland / Sydney
Mexico City / New Delhi / Hong Kong
Danbury, Connecticut

Photo Credits: Cover © L. Clarke/Corbis; pp. 5, 7, 9, 19 © Beste Rowan/Animals Animals; p. 11 © Dave G. Houser/Corbis; p. 13 © Martin Harvey/Corbis; p. 15 © Jim Tuten/Animals Animals; p. 17 © Shoot Pty. Ltd./Index Stock Imagery Inc.; p. 21 © D & J Bartlett/OSF/Animals Animals

Contributing Editor: Shira Laskin
Book Design: Christopher Logan

Library of Congress Cataloging-in-Publication Data

Eckart, Edana.
    Koala / by Edana Eckart.
    p. cm. — (Animals of the world)
    Includes index.
    ISBN 0-516-25053-1 (lib. bdg.) — ISBN 0-516-25164-3 (pbk.)
    1. Koala — Juvenile literature. I. Title.

QL737.M384E34 2005
599.2′5—dc22
                                              2004002351

1 2 3 4 5 6 7 8 9 10 R 14 13 12 11 10 09 08 07 06 05

Contents

Koalas live in **Australia**.

They live in trees.

5

Koalas sleep in the daytime.

Koalas are awake at night.

They eat at night.

Koalas eat the leaves from **eucalyptus** trees.

They eat many leaves every night.

Koalas have two thumbs on their front **paws**.

The thumbs help koalas hold their food and climb trees.

thumbs

Koalas have **thick** fur.

The fur helps koalas stay warm.

Baby koalas are called **joeys**.

The mother koala has a **pouch**.

The joey rides in its mother's pouch after it is born.

Sometimes, a joey rides on its mother's back.

Koalas are amazing animals.

New Words

Australia (aw **strayl**-yuh) a continent in the southeastern part of the world where koalas live

eucalyptus (yoo-kuh-**lip**-tuhss) a very tall tree that grows in dry places, such as Australia

joeys (**joh**-eez) baby koalas

koalas (koh-**ah**-luhz) Australian animals that look like small bears and live in eucalyptus trees

paws (**pawz**) the feet of some animals, such as koalas

pouch (**pouch**) a flap of skin in which koalas and other animals carry their young

thick (**thik**) filling up a lot of space from side to side or from top to bottom

To Find Out More

Books
Koala
by Rod Theodorou
Heinemann Library

The Koala Book
by Ann Sharp
Pelican Publishing Company, Inc.

Web Site
Enchanted Learning: Koala
http://www.EnchantedLearning.com/subjects/mammals/
    marsupial/Koalaprintout.shtml
Print out a picture of a koala to color and learn about
koalas on this Web site.

Index

About the Author
Edana Eckart is a freelance writer. She has written many books about animals.

Reading Consultants
Kris Flynn, Coordinator, Small School District Literacy, The San Diego County
Office of Education

Shelly Forys, Certified Reading Recovery Specialist, W.J. Zahnow Elementary
School, Waterloo, IL

Paulette Mansell, Certified Reading Recovery Specialist, and Early Literacy
Consultant, TX